KU-176-221

Rough Guides

25 Ultimate experiences

Spain

Make the most of your time on Earth

ROUGH GUIDES

25 YEARS 1982–2007

NEW YORK • LONDON • DELHI

Contents

Introduction

EXPERIENCES have always been at the heart of the Rough Guide concept. A group of us began writing the books **25 years ago** (hence this celebratory mini series) and wanted to share the kind of travels we had been doing ourselves. It seems bizarre to recall that in the early 1980s, travel was very much a minority pursuit. Sure, there was a lot of tourism around, and that was reflected in the guidebooks in print, which traipsed around the established sights with scarcely a backward look at the local population and their life. We wanted to change all that: to put a country or a city's popular culture centre stage, to highlight the clubs where you could hear local music, drink with people you hadn't come on holiday with, watch the local football, join in with the festivals. And of course we wanted to push travel a bit further, inspire readers with the confidence and knowledge to break away from established routes, to find pleasure and excitement in remote islands, or desert routes, or mountain treks, or in street culture.

Twenty-five years on, that thinking seems pretty obvious: we all want to experience something real about a destination, and to seek out travel's **ultimate experiences**. Which is exactly where these **25 books** come in. They are not in any sense a new series of guidebooks. We're happy with the series that we already have in print. Instead, the **25s** are a collection of ideas, enthusiasms and inspirations: a selection of the very best things to see or do – and not just before you die, but now. Each selection is gold dust. That's the brief to our writers: there is no room here for the average, no space fillers. Pick any one of our selections and you will enrich your travelling life.

But first of all, take the time to browse. Grab a half dozen of these books and let the ideas percolate ... and then begin making your plans.

Mark Ellingham
Founder & Series Editor, Rough Guides

25

Ultimate
experiences
Spain

In the same way Glasgow outlived a grimy past to become the darling of America's travel media, Bilbao gambled on the cultural dollar and won. By becoming the first European city to fully embrace New York's Guggenheim franchise, it transformed itself from a briny, rusting behemoth into a modern art mecca. Frank O. Gehry's brief was to draw the gaze of the world; his reply was an audacious, ingenious conflation of Bilbao's past and future, a riverine citadel moulded from titanium and limestone, steel and glass. Up close it appears as an urban planner's daydream gone delightfully wrong; viewed from the opposite bank of the river it assumes the guise of a gilded, glittering ark. But it all depends on your mood and the notoriously unpredictable Basque weather: on other days it broods like a computer-generated *Marie Celeste*, or glints rudely like a capricious cross between Monty Python and El Dorado. Gehry extends the aquatic

Gawping at the Guggenheim

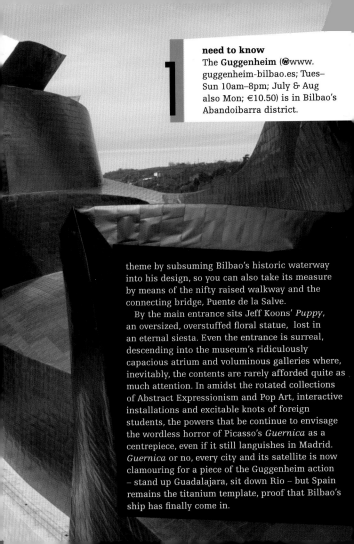

need to know
The **Guggenheim** (Ⓦwww.
guggenheim-bilbao.es; Tues–
Sun 10am–8pm; July & Aug
also Mon; €10.50) is in Bilbao's
Abandoibarra district.

theme by subsuming Bilbao's historic waterway
into his design, so you can also take its measure
by means of the nifty raised walkway and the
connecting bridge, Puente de la Salve.

By the main entrance sits Jeff Koons' *Puppy*,
an oversized, overstuffed floral statue, lost in
an eternal siesta. Even the entrance is surreal,
descending into the museum's ridiculously
capacious atrium and voluminous galleries where,
inevitably, the contents are rarely afforded quite as
much attention. In amidst the rotated collections
of Abstract Expressionism and Pop Art, interactive
installations and excitable knots of foreign
students, the powers that be continue to envisage
the wordless horror of Picasso's *Guernica* as a
centrepiece, even if it still languishes in Madrid.
Guernica or no, every city and its satellite is now
clamouring for a piece of the Guggenheim action
– stand up Guadalajara, sit down Rio – but Spain
remains the titanium template, proof that Bilbao's
ship has finally come in.

Watching
Real Madrid

Picture the Queen schmoozing Tony Blair at Old Trafford; difficult, isn't it? In Spain, politics, royalty and football have always mixed more freely. Not only did General Franco infamously adopt Real Madrid as the de facto sporting wing of his regime, but King Juan Carlos counselled Spain's first post-Franco prime minister during a game with Saragossa. These days, it's the players who get the red carpet treatment, and Real Madrid – now a billion-dollar brand and one of the biggest sport franchises in the world – can boast the bluest blooded line-up of all. Real's underperforming *Galácticos* may have been royally humbled in recent times, but on a good day they can still dribble, shoot and shimmy like the fantasy football team they are. You can see them up close at the Bernabéu, Real's majestic – Fifa describe it as "mythical" – 80,000 capacity stadium named after the president who masterminded it, which has witnessed such grand sporting occasions as the Euro 1964 final (when Franco's Spain snatched victory from the USSR) and the 1982 World Cup final.

It's an imposing place, one where you can sense history seeping through the concrete, right to your seemingly vertically tiered plastic seat. Don't be surprised if many of them remain empty as kick-off draws near: the legendary Spanish tardiness means no one likes to turn up too soon. Besides, you wouldn't want to miss the pre-match atmosphere in the surrounding bars – even the obligatory Irish pub is ablaze with Real colours. Fans may not make as much noise as you'd expect, but – if their team isn't cutting it – they'll soon whip out their famous white hankies. Real Madrid's superstar cachet and the huge number of season ticket holders means most matches are sell-outs, but you can always console yourself with a tour of their bulging trophy cabinets.

at the
Bernabéu

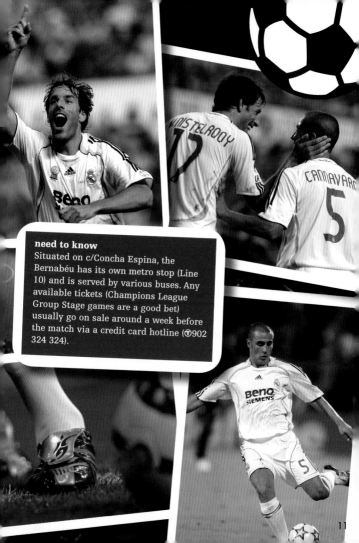

need to know

Situated on c/Concha Espina, the Bernabéu has its own metro stop (Line 10) and is served by various buses. Any available tickets (Champions League Group Stage games are a good bet) usually go on sale around a week before the match via a credit card hotline (☎902 324 324).

Living without sleep in
Valencia

3

need to know
For an excellent overview of what's hot pick up a free copy of the English-language listings guide *24-7 Valencia* (Ⓦwww.thisisvalencia.com) or the clubbier Spanish-language *alb* (*A Little Beat*).

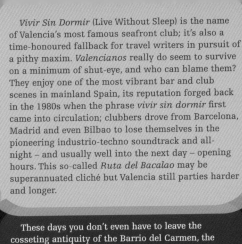

Vivir Sin Dormir (Live Without Sleep) is the name of Valencia's most famous seafront club; it's also a time-honoured fallback for travel writers in pursuit of a pithy maxim. *Valencianos* really do seem to survive on a minimum of shut-eye, and who can blame them? They enjoy one of the most vibrant bar and club scenes in mainland Spain, its reputation forged back in the 1980s when the phrase *vivir sin dormir* first came into circulation; clubbers drove from Barcelona, Madrid and even Bilbao to lose themselves in the pioneering industrio-techno soundtrack and all-night – and usually well into the next day – opening hours. This so-called *Ruta del Bacalao* may be superannuated cliché but Valencia still parties harder and longer.

These days you don't even have to leave the cosseting antiquity of the Barrio del Carmen, the hugely atmospheric old town where vintage tapas joints rub shoulders with post-modern tea shops, live jazz locks horns with bpms and each dimly lit lane holds the promise of something funky. Once the domain of the infamous Borgia clan, the central Calle Caballeros now plays host to a boisterous cross section of mullet-headed locals, fur-lined theatre-goers, fresh-faced Erasmus students and *guiris* (foreign tourists) of every stripe. Many of their paths cross at *Radio City*, a bohemian cauldron of live theatre and dance. Flamenco and world music fans can indulge in the village-hall-style intimacy of *Café Del Duende* and *La Bodegueta*, a haunt of legends like Paco de Lucia. Valencia also boasts Spain's biggest salsa scene, situated to the south of Carmen around Plaza de España, where clubs like *Gran Caimán* and *Glamour de Bachata* are within swinging distance of each other. *Bounty* and *Pinball* are both excellent boltholes for funk-soul luddites, and when the Barrio does eventually wind down around 4am, hardened clubbers need only nip across town to *Latex*, *Piccadilly* or the recently opened branch of superclub *Pacha*, all of which will shake your booty till breakfast time.

Granada:
Exploring the
Alhambra

Towering out of an elm-wooded hillside above Granada, a snow-dusted Sierra Nevada behind, there are few more iconic images of Spain than the ochre-tinted enclave of the Alhambra. By the time the last Moorish prince, Boabdil, was scolded (by his mother) with the immortal line "Do not weep like a woman for what you could not defend like a man", a succession of Nasrid rulers had expanded upon the bare bones of the Alcazaba (or citadel). In doing so they created an exalted wonder of the temporal world, elevating its inhabitants with voluptuous waterways and liberating inscriptions.

Yet its contemporary status as the country's most revered monument is due at least in part to Washington Irving, a sometime American diplomat in Madrid better known for writing *The Legend Of Sleepy Hollow*. In the mid-nineteenth century, at a time when no one gave the place a second glance, Irving recognized its faded glamour, completing his *Tales of the Alhambra* in the abandoned palace.

Now over five thousand visitors wander through the restored complex every day, its chambers and gardens once again alive with cosmopolitan chatter if not free-flowing verse. No amount of words, however, can approximate the sensual charge of witnessing the Palacios Nazaries for the first time, the best preserved palace of the Nasrid dynasty. As a building the palace's function was to concentrate the mind on the oneness of God, and nowhere is this more apparent than the Patio de los Leones courtyard. Here Arabic calligraphy sweeps across the stucco with unparalleled grace, stalactite vaulting dazzles in its intricate irregularity and white marble lions guard a symbolic representation of paradise. The sweet irony is that none of it was built to last, its elementary adobe and wood in harmony with the elements and in stark contrast to the Alcazaba fortress opposite, the impregnable looking towers of which have defined the Granada skyline for centuries.

need to know
The Alhambra is open March–Oct daily 8.30am–8pm, also Tues–Sat 10–11.30pm; Nov–Feb daily 8.30am–6pm, Fri & Sat also 8–9.30pm; €10. Advance booking recommended (Ⓦ www .alhambratickets .com).

In any account of the Extremadura region's history, a neat parallel is usually drawn between the austerity of the landscape and the savagery of the conquistadores born and raised there. Its alternately broiling and bitterly cold plains hold an empty allure that's hard to shake off, and the contrast with its towns is striking. Both Trujillo and Cáceres remain synonymous with *conquistador* plunder, rich in lavish *solares* (mansions) built by New World returnees. Cáceres is UNESCO-protected, but Trujillo is even prettier, its sons more infamous. This was the birthplace of Francisco Pizarro, illiterate conqueror of Peru and scourge of the Incas.

While a bronze likeness coolly surveys the Plaza Mayor, the legacy of his less bloodthirsty half-brother bother, Hernando, is more imposing: the Palacio de la Conquista lords it over the square, its richly ornamented facade adorned with a doomed Atahualpa and spuriously sage-looking busts of both Pizarro siblings – the ultimate expression of local hombres made good. Nearby is the Palacio de Orellana-Pizarro, transformed from a fortress into a *conquistador*'s des res by Francisco's cousin Juan, and crowned by an exquisite Renaissance balcony.

Need to know Most mansions are restricted to exterior viewing. WOMAD (Ⓦ www.womad.org) is held during the first fortnight in May, with Tinariwen, Susana Baca and Talvin Singh all appearing in recent years.

Keeping it in the family was equally important in Cáceres: the town's most impressive mansion, the Casa de Toledo-Moctezuma, is a work of mannerist indulgence and august grandeur, a place with royal Aztec connections where the son of *conquistador* Juan Cano (an acolyte of Hernán Cortés) and Doña Isabel (daughter of the Mexican emperor) settled down with his Spanish bride. Across the old town, the gorgeous honeyed-gothic facade of the Casa de los Golfines de Abajo dates back to the years immediately prior to the New World voyages.

These days, the wealth of the Indies arrives in the form of sweet music asthe world music jamboree that is WOMAD flings open its doors in Cáceres for four days each May. With consummate irony then, it's possible to bask in balmy Latin American sounds, surrounded by mansions financed by Latin American gold.

Discovering the Conquistadors' Spoils

Defining the topography of Asturias and Cantabria, and even nudging into León, the Parque Nacional Picos de Europa throws a lot of limestone weight around for a comparatively compact range.

It's also **stubbornly diverse** and **disarmingly magnificent**, long the destination of choice for not only discerning European trekkers and climbers but also cavers, who are drawn to the 1km-plus depths of its tentacle-like drainage system. Much like the parks of northern Portugal, the Picos shelter countless stone-clad villages and hamlets which the land has sustained for centuries and where the trekking industry is comparatively recent. But the layered vista of beech-forested valleys, **flinty summer pasture** and incongruous **lunar peaks** makes the range particularly alluring and **deceptively benign**. The history likewise generates its own **mystique**, literally enshrined in stone at the pilgrimage site of Covadonga on the park's far western fringe. This was where, in the early eighth century, the beleaguered Christians allegedly took their first Moorish scalp and **kick-started** the Reconquista. You don't have to be a believer to appreciate the Picos, although a sense of **divine presence** might help, especially in negotiating the **forbidding**, 1.5km-deep chasm that is the Cares Gorge. It remains the **definitive Picos experience**, usually accessed from the village of Caín, from whence the most impressive bridges and tunnels are in easy reach. As **griffon vultures tailspin** high overhead, well-fed day-trippers and the occasional heavily laden hiker pick their way along a path **audaciously gouged** out of the cliff face. The gorge forms a natural boundary between the less visited western mountains and the central massif where the official daddy of the Picos, Torre Cerredo, is outclassed by its rakish, **orange-bronzed rival**, the Naranjo de Bulnes. The Naranjo is a perennial favourite with climbers, however even they've been known to succumb to the less arduous thrill of the *teleférico* as it **shudders up** more than 750 metres of sheer cliff.

need to know

The main park office in Oviedo, c/Arquitecto Reguera 13 (☎985 241 412, ⓦwww.picoseuropa.net) has Spanish-only info on routes and accommodation. ⓦwww.asturiaspicosdeeuropa.com is a useful English-language site maintained by expat hoteliers.

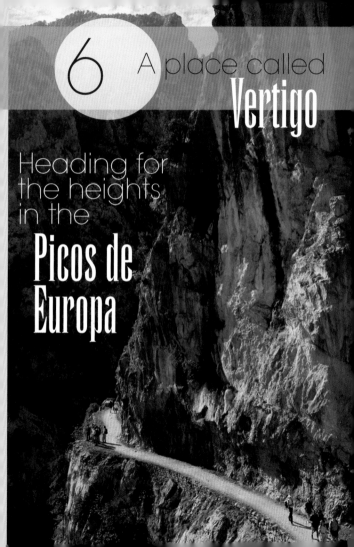

6 A place called Vertigo

Heading for the heights in the

Picos de Europa

7

RUNNING
WITH THE BULLS IN
PAMPLONA

For one week each year the Spanish town of Pamplona parties so hard that the foothills of the nearby Pyrenees start shaking. The scariest, loudest and most raucous party you'll ever come across, the Fiesta de San Fermin, held in honour of Pamplona's patron saint, has been celebrated since the early sixteenth century. But it's the daily ritual of the notoriously dangerous *encierro* or bull run – the most prominent feature of the event for at least two hundred years and something of a rite of passage for young men of the region – that gets all the attention.

Nothing can prepare you for your first Pamplona experience: the constant flow of beer and sangria, the outrageous drunken partying, the hordes of excited people in the streets, and, most of all, the early morning terror of the bull run. It only lasts about three-and-a-half minutes but is pure adrenaline all the way, with half-a-dozen bulls running 800m or so to the town's main bullring behind several thousand would-be heroes. The first bull run is held on the morning of July 7, after which the ritual of all-night partying followed by a morning bull run followed by a few hours sleep is repeated until July 14, when there's a solemn closing ceremony. There are also bullfights every evening, a naked procession to protest at the cruelty of the whole event and regular drunken diving from one of the statues in the main square. You've got to hand it to the Spanish – they certainly know how to host a phenomenal party.

need to know
The first thing to do when you arrive is to head for Plaza del Castillo to the mobile tourist office for a timetable of events and your free map. The official website Ⓦ www.sanfermin.com has more information.

Sun, sea and ski: it just doesn't sound right.

Yet Spain is the second highest landmass in Europe next to Switzerland, boasting more than five times as many resorts as Scotland. The most southerly resort in Europe, the Sierra Nevada warily eyes Africa across the Mediterranean. Its often erratic snow conditions aren't the greatest but the t-shirt temperatures and dearth of attitude are a breath of fresh mountain air.

More than anything, though, the lure of Andalucían skiing lies in its location, in the glorious novelty of sunning yourself on the Cabo de Gata in the morning and going on the piste in the afternoon. Its height – the towering Mulhacén stands at well over 3500 metres – is another factor: as late as May, when resorts further north are covered in Alpine grass and trekkers, skiing is still an option.

At heart, the resort is a beginner's playground, with miles of gentle piste and special "magic carpet" conveyor lifts. If you've ever squinted through a howling wall of Glenshee sleet, or had your legs embarrassingly part company with your tow at a 45-degree angle, you'll appreciate Sierra Nevada's undulating rhythm and sapphire skies.

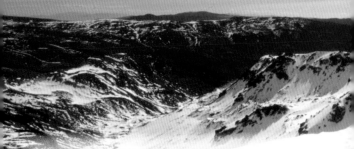

If such wimpish gradients are anathema, or you like your snow a little more stylish, head for the swanky, relatively remote resort of Baqueira-Beret in Catalunya's Vall d'Aran. A morning dip on the Costa Brava will mean getting up a hell of lot earlier, but as a haunt of Spain's great and good, the place boasts the Catalan Pyrenees' best facilities and most challenging pick of pine-dotted pistes.

Intermediates with a taste for Atlantic weather should seek out the modern Cantabrian resort of Alto Campoo. The number of lifts and tows barely makes it into double figures but the resort's tranquillity and unassuming beauty renders it increasingly popular. Whichever resort you choose, enjoy it while it lasts – global warming looks likely to hit the industry hard.

skiing
under a
Spanish
sun

8

need to know
Sierra Nevada Ski
Station (Ⓦwww.
sierranevadaski.com) is
32km north of Granada.
The Spanish aversion
to queuing means
weekends, Christmas
and Easter are probably
best avoided. Check
Ⓦwww.baqueira.es
for up to date info on
Banqueira-Beret.

Given that Galicia's patron saint was originally a fisherman, it's only right that the place serves up some of the best seafood in the world. Its *rias* (inlets), are filled with the kind of fishy abundance that Steve Zissou would trade his red beanie for; a life aquatic numbering gourmet varieties of scallops, eel, clams, mussels, prawns, lobster and crabs, many of which end up in local restaurant windows. The rugged, world's end coast further north, meanwhile, nurtures such outlandish delicacies as the digit-like *percebes*, or goose-barnacle. Like a modern day equivalent to the St Kilda egg collectors, *percebeiros* gather these oddly obscene looking creatures from wave-lashed rocks, risking life and limb for what the Spanish – and clued-up foreign foodies – consider manna from the ocean. If you sample them amidst the chandeliers and sharp suits of a Madrid institution like *Casa Rafa*, you'll pay two or three times what you would for freshly gathered specimens in Galicia itself (you might even get a free tasting at O Grove's shellfish festival); either way they're boiled and eaten as they are, so not a single molecule of luscious, gulf stream-pure flavour is lost.

Pulpo addiction:

9

Cheaper and much more abundant is *pulpo a la gallega*, a characteristically simple yet ravishing dish of boiled, chopped octopus dressed with olive oil, crusty sea salt and sweet, pungent *pimentón* (paprika), served at earthy specialist eateries called *pulperías*. As *pulpo á feira*, it's usually the dish of choice at the region's many festivals and the sole focus of a summer bash in Carballiño, near Ourense, where hefty, flame-haired Galician matriarchs man copper urns and serve their wares on wooden platters.

need to know

Santiago de Compostela's Rúa do Franco is lined with great seafood places and almost every Galician town has a decent *pulpería*. For some of the best *percebes*, try the hamlet of San Andrés de Teixido or the nearby port of Cedeira. Further down the coast, O Grove is another seafood paradise; the shellfish festival usually runs for a week, starting on the second Sunday in October. Carballiño's octopus festival is held on the second Sunday in August.

GOING GASTRO IN GALICIA

10

Surreal Life at the Dalí Museum

"He had problems with his sexuality, you know," "Aye, the tree represents impotence."

Such overheard snatches of **amateur Freudianism** are what you might expect at the **Teatre-Museu Dalí**; nothing, however, can ready you for the sheer volume of outwardly respectable, smart-casual tourists crowding desperately around the **unwholesome creations** of Catalonia's most eccentric, outrageous and egotistical son. Within a **salmon pink**, egg-topped palace ("like Elton John's holiday home", quipped one visitor) in the heart of **Figueres**, class and generation gaps dissolve as young and old strain to aim their cameras at a siren-like Queen of Persia **riding barefoot** atop an Al Capone car. In the back seat very wet and hollow chested passengers look like they have tussled with **Day Of The Triffids** just one time too many. As the **irreverence** of the exhibits triggers an irreverence of the spirit, standard gallery politesse goes out the window. A **funhouse-like frisson** takes its place as frumpy pensioners queue to climb a staircase and **gape** at a distorted approximation of **Mae West's face**; gangling students make what they will of an incongruous Duke Ellington album sleeve, an **Alice Cooper hologram** and a gilded monkey skeleton; and designer-tagged *señoritas* **jostle** for a good position to crane their necks, point and click at a **kitschy**, fleshy footed self-portrait **reaching for the heavens**. Even if you're only dimly aware of Dalí's liquified Surrealism, an hour in the man's domain will convince you that **queasy paintings** like the candle-faced *Cosmic Athletes* were dredged from one of the most singular subconscious minds of the twentieth century, one unhitched from the Surrealist vanguard in favour of his own, brilliantly christened "paranoiac-critical" method. Like Gaudí before him, Salvador Dalí's monument was also his last, **reclusive** refuge. The man is actually buried in the crypt, right below your feet, and it's easy to imagine his **moustachioed ghost** prowling the half-moon corridors, **bug-eyed and impish**, revelling in the knowledge that his **lurid mausoleum** is Spain's most sought after **art spectacular** after the Prado.

need to know

The museum is open daily: June 10.30am–6pm; July–Sept 9am–8pm; Oct–May Tues–Sun 10.30am–6pm; €10; Ⓦwww.salvador-dali.org.

11

Cruising through the

The supposed site of the lost city of Atlantis, the preserve of the Duchess of Alba, Goya's muse, and a favourite hunting haunt of seventeenth-century monarchs Felipe IV and Felipe V, Andalucía's Coto de Doñana was also, up until recently, the infamous domain of malaria-carrying mosquitos.

While many of Spain's wetland areas were drained in the fight against the disease, which put paid to many a royal and was only eradicated in1964, the swampy triangle that is the Rio Guadalquivir delta escaped with its water and wildlife intact. Five years after the area was declared disease free, almost 350 square kilometres came under the aegis of the Parque Nacional de Doñana, Spain's largest national park. Today, the area is both a UNESCO World Heritage Site and Biosphere Reserve, and encompasses more than 770 square kilometres. Illuminated by the hallucinatory glare of the Costa de la Luz sun, it's a place of tart

need to know
Daily four-hour bus tours depart from the reception centre at El Acebuche, 4km north of the coastal resort of Matalascañas (☎959 430 432). River trips are available from Sanlúcar de Barrameda (☎956 363 644).

Coto de Doñana

air and buckled horizons, with that almost mystical lure encountered in unbroken landscapes.

Bordered by the urban centres of Seville, Huelva and Cádiz, it suffers under the kind of man-made encroachments from which remoter parks are immune, so it's likely your visit will be confined to a guided tour in an incongruously militaristic 4WD bus. Yet as your driver barrels past sand dunes, sun-blind lagoons and pine stands with typically brusque abandon, you can rest easy in the knowledge that the flamingos, wild boar, tortoise, red deer, mongoose and vultures that reside here are otherwise left in peace. Eking out a living alongside them are small, endangered populations of imperial eagles and Iberian lynx, as well as a rude array of migratory birds that alight in flooded marshes on their way back from West Africa in winter and spring. How many of them you actually see will depend on luck, season and a good pair of binoculars; just remember to pack that repellent.

The only genuine desert in Europe, Almería's merciless canyons and moonscape gulches did, once upon a time in the **Spanish Wild West**, play host to **Hollywood**. Back in the Sixties, Spaghetti Western don **Sergio Leone** shot his landmark trilogy here, climaxing with *The Good, The Bad & The Ugly*. Since this **golden era** the place has had an occasional flash of former glories: in the mid-Eighties **Alex Cox** revisited the terrain with his all-star spaghetti parody *Straight To Hell*, and **Sean Connery** pitched up for *Indiana Jones and the Last Crusade*.

As recently as 2002, Spanish director Alex de la Iglesia's critically acclaimed *800 Bullets* actually subsumed Almerían cinema's rise and fall into its plot, centring on the **Fort Bravo studios/Texas Hollywood**, where the **most authentic** film-set experience is still to be had. It's a gloriously eerie, **down at heel** place, which, likely as not, you'll have to yourself. Unfortunately, there's no explanation as to which sets were used in which films but the splintered wood, fading paintwork and general dilapidation certainly feels genuine. A wholesale Mexican compound complete with blinding white mission chapel is the atmospheric centrepiece; close your eyes and you can just about **smell the gunpowder**. The saloon is the very same one that David Beckham stalked through in a 2003 TV ad, where the cream of Real Madrid fortified themselves on Pepsi before a showdown with the Manchester United squad.

A couple of kilometres down the road is **Mini-Hollywood**, the sanitized big daddy of the region's three film-set theme parks, with a must-see museum of original poster art. And Leone diehards will want to complete the tour with a visit to nearby **Western Leone**, which houses the extant debris of the man's masterpiece, *Once Upon A Time In The West*. Hopeless cowboys (and girls) can even take a four day horse-riding tour into the desert, scouting various locations amid **breathtakingly desiccated**

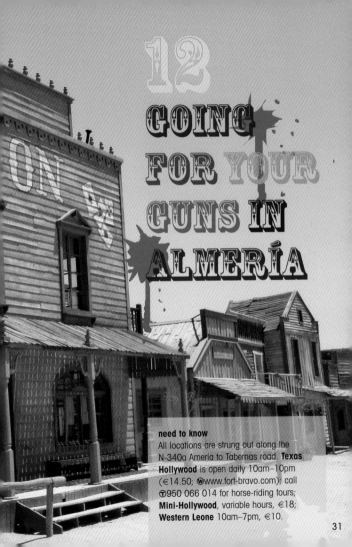

12 GOING FOR YOUR GUNS IN ALMERÍA

need to know

All locations are strung out along the N-340a Amería to Tabernas road. **Texas Hollywood** is open daily 10am–10pm (€14.50; ⓦwww.fort-bravo.com); call ☎950 066 014 for horse-riding tours; **Mini-Hollywood**, variable hours, €18; **Western Leone** 10am–7pm, €10.

Land of the rising vine:
The bold sights
and subtle flavours of
La Rioja

13

Oak-toasty, berry-pungent Rioja wine has been the pride of Spain for centuries.

It's a tipple that the Castillian court appreciated sufficiently to issue quasi-protectionist decrees as early as the twelfth century, but, with French know how, only really began assuming its contemporary character in the 1850s. Having retreated to Bordeaux to escape political unrest at home, one Camilo Hurtado de Amézaga, otherwise known as

Marqués de Riscal, returned to northern Spain armed with vines, oak casks and an amateur's enthusiasm, and pioneered classic, oak-aged Rioja with his own bodega in the town of Elciego.

More than a century and a half later, the Marqués de Riscal dynasty is pioneering another seismic shift, and

precipitating mass enotourism with a Frank O. Gehry-designed City Of Wine. Topped by leaves of lilac- and gold-tinted steel, transposing vines into modern art, the complex incorporates a hotel, restaurant, museum and even a trendy spa. Not that they're the first bodega to hire a hip architect: the strikingly situated and designed Bodegas Ysios, near the hill town of Laguardia is the work of Santiago Calatrava. It is an aluminium Mexican wave of a building housing a wine acclaimed for its fruit-driven complexity.

Other bodegas have invested the shock of the new solely in their finished product – places like Roda in Haro, the slightly dowdy but charming viticultural hub in the region's far northwest. Strategically planned and purpose-built, Roda painstakingly fine tunes its winemaking process, selecting old-vine grapes for their celebrated, tannin-rich Cirsión range. Still dedicated to traditional oak fermentation is Haro's Muga, a wonderful old bodega down by the town's train station where they crack open eggs by the hundred, using the white to filter the wine, and where you can watch reticent-looking artisans crafting in-house barrels.

need to know
Marques de Riscal tours are bookable in advance (€6; ⓦwww.marquesderiscal .com); **Roda** (ⓦwww.roda.es) and **Ysios** (ⓦwww.byb.es) by appointment; **Muga**'s tours in English Mon–Fri 10am (ⓦwww.bodegasmuga.com; € 5).

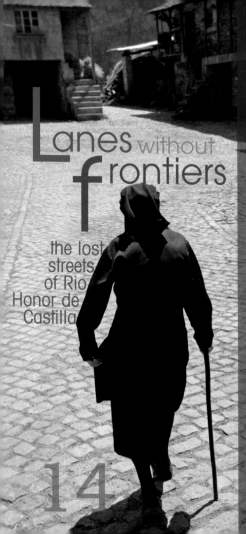

Lanes without frontiers

the lost streets of Rio Honor de Castilla

14

Long before Spanish–Portuguese borders were abandoned to EU integration and the elements, the good folk of Rio Honor de Castilla/Rio de Onor lived as though they'd never existed. Isolated at the tip of Spain's Old Castille and Portugal's Trás-Os-Montes regions these two villages-in-one effectively ignored political frontiers while the rest of Europe tore itself apart. Nowadays any lawbreaking that goes on is subject to respective national laws rather than the traditional fines in wine, but the unique egalitarian systems and language (Rionorês, a hybrid of Portuguese and the Castillian dialect of Leonese) stan as a testament to the absurdity of arbitrary division.

Though the young people have long departed, the old ways survive and there's a tangible sense that things have always been done differently:

need to know
Rio Honor de Castilla/
Rio de Onor is 12km
from the Leonese fortress
town of Puebla de
Sanabria; taxis (☎980
620 301) regularly
make the 20-minute trip.
Clean and comfortable
accommodation is
available in the **Casa
do Povo** for around
€20; contact the village
presidente on ☎273
927 128, or ask for
directions to his house.

in contrast to neighbouring villages, the leathery, black-clad elders are garrulous and inquisitive. They still tend a central plot of land and lead their animals through dung-clotted streets, stabling them below their sagging schist houses. The few narrow streets on either side of the settlement are among the most haunting in the whole of the Iberian peninsula; untold years of cross-cultural birth, life, work and death linger in the mountain air, even as the population peters out.

If you're linguistically equipped, you can savour the novelty of speaking Portuguese in the tiny, ancient bar and Castillian in the grocery store where, true to type, the owner – not so used to the company of *guiris* – can talk for Spain (or should that be Portugal?). A stone bridge is all that separates the two villages; how long they can work together to stave off the ravages of depopulation is another question. For now at least, though, Rio Honor de Castilla/Rio de Onor is a fascinating, hugely atmospheric step back in time and a fading glimpse of a world without borders.

TAPAS
CRAWLING
IN THE CAPITAL

15

Tapas crawling is to the Spaniard what pub crawling is to the northern European, with the added bonus that you're not literally crawling by the end of the night, or at least you shouldn't be if you've faithfully scoffed a tidbit with each drink.

In Granada and assorted hinterlands they're still a complimentary courtesy; in the rest of the country a free lunch has gone the way of the siesta and the peseta. But if you're going to pay for your nibbles, Madrid offers one of the meanest tapas crawls in the land, starting from the central Puerta del Sol. In and around the narrow streets between Sol and Plaza Santa Ana you can tuck into fluffy fried prawns and erm...

more prawns (*al ajillo*, in garlic), washed down by heady house wine at the Lilliputian *Casa del Abuelo*. Unpretentious, atmospheric bars also serving authentic bites are *Las Bravas*, a former barbers turned fried-potato-in-spicy-sauce specialist with a closely guarded recipe, and *La Oreja de Oro*, which translates as "the golden ear", but in fact serves ears of the conspicuously edible variety. The fried pigs' parts are a concession to local tastes, the rest of the menu – including Ribeiro wine served in bowls and *pimientos de Padrón* (unpredictably hot fried peppers) – wearing its Galician colours proudly. If cartilage doesn't tickle your tastebuds, it's probably worth taking a little detour back to the western edge of the Plaza Mayor for *Mesón del Champiñones*, an earthy taberna that's been doling out mouthwatering pan-fried mushrooms and sangría for longer than most *Madrileños* can remember. Even older is *Taberna de Antonio Sanchez* in nearby Lavapiés, a venerable bullfighters' den dating from 1830, where the dark wood walls are heavy with scarred taurine trophies from long forgotten duels. For something less queasy to finish up, cut back east to *Taberna de Dolores* on Plaza de Jesús, where the slender Roquefort and anchovy canapés will ensure you wake up with fearsome breath, if not a hangover.

need to know

Casa del Abuelo
c/Victoria 12.

Las Bravas
c/Alvarez Gato 3.

La Oreja de Oro
c/Victoria 9.

Mesón del Champiñones
Cava de San Miguel 17.

Taberna de Antonio Sánchez
c/Mesón de Paredes 13.

Taberna de Dolores
Plaza de Jesús 4.

The Gaudí Complex:

on the trail of Barcelona's strangest buildings

16

In Iberia's long, art-historical legacy of overstatement, the one wobbly vision that never ceases to fascinate is that of Antoni Gaudí i Cornet, a God-fearing eccentric in a city of anarchist agitation and the unlikeliest of Catalan champions. His contribution to Modernisme, the Catalan version of Art Nouveau, was particularly rarefied, recognizing no obstacle in expressing the organic complexity of a world his God had so painstakingly created.

His timing also lacked earthly constraints, ensuring his masterpiece, the Sagrada Família, would still be under construction when church-burning anarchism was a sacrilegious memory. In terms of Barcelona's cultural heritage, the Sagrada Família is the writhing, biomorphic pinnacle of both Gaudí's own UNESCO World Heritage-flagged works and the city's wider architectural cachet. Its apostolic towers thrust into the sky northeast of the famous L'Eixample, the district where Modernista architects were given free reign by their industrialist patrons.

Further west on the elegant Passeig de Gràcia lie two of the most infamous of Gaudí's secular designs. Or at least the Casa Milà used to be infamous, locals taking such exception to its heaving undulations that they disparagingly dubbed it La Pedrera: the quarry. The nickname stuck but now it's a must-see stop on the Gaudí trail, admired for its balconied ribbons of wrought-iron seaweed and outlandish, almost reptilian roof sculptures. The shark-eyed balconies, stone lips and dazzling ceramics of nearby Casa Batlló likewise render it an inert gatecrasher at some long-forgotten masked ball.

Then there's the random excess of Parc Güell, a mindbending, free-to-enter garden of delights with upended stone palm trunks and a psychedelic lizard. Perhaps the greatest aspect of Gaudí's work is its fluidity, its refusal to be defined; what one observer regards as an aquatic mass, another sees as a cave-studded, snow-capped mountain. Gaudí has been proposed for sainthood, but wherever his spirit lingers surely can't be quite as fantastical as the stonescapes he imagined on earth.

need to know

You can see the genius of Gaudí's facades for free but it's worth paying for closer inspection: **Sagrada Família** daily: April–Sept 9am–8pm; Oct–March 9am–6pm; €8. **Casa Milà** daily 10am–8pm; €8. **Casa Batlló** daily 9am–8pm; €16. **Parc Güell** daily: March & Oct 10am–7pm; April & Sept 10am–8pm; May–Aug 10am–9pm; Nov–Feb 10am–6pm.

17 PREY MACARENA

The Spanish flock may be wavering but, being Catholic and proud, they take their religious festivals as seriously as they did in the days when a pointy hat meant the Inquisition. Semana Santa (or Holy Week) is the most spectacular of all the Catholic celebrations, and Seville carries it off with an unrivalled pomp and ceremony. Conceived as an extravagant antidote to Protestant asceticism, the festivities were originally designed to steep the common man in Christ's Passion, and it's the same today – the dazzling climax to months of preparation. You don't need to be a Christian to appreciate the outlandish spectacle or the exquisitely choreographed attention to detail. Granted, if you're not expecting it, the sight of massed hooded penitents can

be disorientating and not a little disturbing – rows of eyes opaque with concentration, feet stepping slavishly in time with brass and percussion. But Holy Week is also about the *pasos* or floats, elaborate slow-motion platforms graced with piercing, tottering images of Jesus

and the Virgin Mary, swathed in *Sevillano* finery. All across Seville, crowds hold their collective breath as they anticipate the moment when their local church doors are thrown back

Easter in Seville

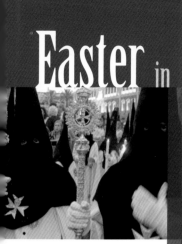

From here they proceed to the cathedral, where on Good Friday morning the whole thing reaches an ecstatic climax with the appearance of *La Macarena*, the protector of Seville's bullfighters long before she graced the pop charts.

and the *paso* commences its unsteady journey, the *costaleros* (or bearers) sweating underneath, hidden from view. With almost sixty *cofradías*, or brotherhoods, all mounting their own processions between Palm Sunday and Good Friday, the city assumes the guise of a sacred snakes-and-ladders board, criss-crossed by caped, candle-lit columns at all hours of the day and night, heavy with the ambrosial scent of incense and orange blossom, and pierced by the plaintive lament of the *saetas*, unaccompanied flights of religious song sung by locals on their balconies. Regardless of where the processions start they all converge on c/Sierpes, the commercial thoroughfare jammed with families who've paid for a front-seat view.

need to know
The official Semana Santa programme of events is available from newstands; local newspapers also print timetables and route maps.

41

The wind on the plain blows mostly in Spain, and there's no Spanish town more synonymous with wind than Tarifa. Facing down Morocco across the Gibraltar Straits, it's both a windsurfing magnet and a suicide blackspot where the relentless gusting can literally drive people mad. But don't let that put you off; you're more likely to be driven to distraction in the concrete inferno of Costas Brava, Blanca or Sol, an orgy of development from which the Costa de la Luz has thus far abstained.

In contrast, Tarifa is a whitewashed rendezvous, a chimerical canvas where the Med meets the Atlantic, the Poniente wind meets the Levante and Africa meets Europe. Even as body-built windsurfers ride the tide and live large, the Rif Mountains of *kif* farms and Paul Bowles-imagined Gothic loom across the waves like emissaries of another, darker star.

Climactic conditions for wind- and kitesurfing are optimal in the afternoon and early evening once the Levante hits its stride, although beginners are usually schooled in the morning. There are several rental places in Tarifa itself, and other facilities farther up the crescent of bleached-sand beach. When the sun goes down, Tangier's lights start beckoning, and it is possible (just) to get your afternoon's surfing fix

18

TARIFA

TANGIER

before heading to Morocco for the evening, avoiding the daytime scrum of quayside touts, and arriving just as sunset breathes new energy into the city's pavement cafés.

   Stumbling into a harshly day-lit street from a hotel you entered in darkness, the culture shock hits hard. Despite its seedy reputation, Tangier is a fascinating place, where you can meditate over William Burroughs and mint tea, take an incorrigibly polite tour of an Anglican church, zone out on *gnawa* music and make the medina *muezzin* your dawn alarm. And once you've experienced Morocco, the sight of Tarifa's harbour walls and bulging sails on your return seems even more illusory, more a continuation of North Africa than an outpost of Europe.

need to know
Spin Out Surf Base (@www.tarifaspinout.com) rent equipment for €25 per hour. FRS (@www.frs.es) run fast ferries (35min) between Tarifa and Tangier up to seven times a day.

Surfing the Coast
Of Light
Crossing the Gibraltar
Straits from Tarifa to
Tangier

To be a Pilgrim 19
El Camino de Santiago

We all know God works in mysterious ways; one of his most mysterious is the way he manages to wrest Spaniards away from their sedentary lifestyles and into the hinterlands of the north: a surprising seventy percent of people following the Way of Saint James are native. Some may be genuine staff-clasping, scallop-bearing pilgrims in search of a pardon from purgatory, on their way to prostrate themselves before Saint James' mortal remains. More are likely to be tourists in their own land, in search of Romanesque churches, untamed scenery and an indelible sense of the arcane.

The route's been tramped since the tenth century, and by the middle ages the Camino was clocking up half a million culturally diverse pilgrims per year, converging from as far afield as Paris, London and Rome, prompting Goethe to declare that "Europe was formed journeying to Santiago." Dubbed *el camino francés*, the UNESCO-sponsored stretch that teems with trekkers and cyclists today begins on the lower slopes of the Spanish Pyrenees, where a charged, twelfth-century blessing in the Monastery of Roncesvalles begs celestial protection from the sun and Spanish road signs (well, at least guidance at crossroads). From here, it's a case of follow the yellow arrow road through bottle green Basque pasture, in the hoof steps of Charlemagne, and on to Pamplona, the plains of Castille and the wilds of Galicia, where ancient *pallozas* (thatched stone huts) make the wind-whipped hamlet of Cebreiro an intemperate wonder. If you're on a budget, and mind neither Gregorian-strength snoring or the odd pre-dawn, strip light wake-up call, you can lodge at rudimentary *albergues* along the route. Alternative accommodation is usually available but, by the time you've finally limped into Santiago de Compostela, the *albergues*' communal, multi-lingual spirit will have worked wonders for those blisters.

need to know
The *camino francés* stretches for 750km, beginning in Roncesvalles thirty miles northeast of Pamplona; allow 6–8 weeks. The *albuergues* are regularly spaced and accommodation is usually free or subject to a few euros donation, providing you have a *credencial* (available in advance from a pilgrim association or from Roncesvalles Monastery).

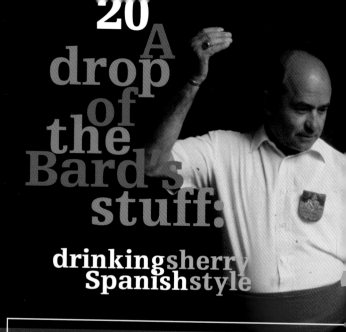

20

A drop of the Bard's stuff:

drinking sherry Spanish style

Sixteenth-century England mightn't been have been so green and pleasant for Spain's Armada but at least the Bard was busy lauding its wine. Falstaff's avowal of the properties of "sherris-sack" should probably be taken with a *pincho* of salt, but there's nothing quite like a chilled glass of *fino* in the Andalucían shade. The vineyards from which it derives are among the oldest on earth, surviving the disapproval of Moorish rulers, the ravages of civil war and a phylloxera epidemic, only to face a twenty-first-century market saturated with trendy New World competition. Downsized but unbowed, they still occupy the famous sherry triangle bounded by the southwestern towns of Jerez de la Frontera, San Lúcar de Barrameda and El Puerto de Santa María, intent on attracting a younger, hipper market. And why not; the sickly cream sherries

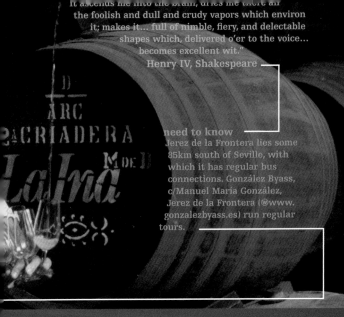

It ascends me into the brain, dries me there all
the foolish and dull and crudy vapors which environ
it; makes it... full of nimble, fiery, and delectable
shapes which, delivered o'er to the voice...
becomes excellent wit.'
Henry IV, Shakespeare

need to know
Jerez de la Frontera lies some
85km south of Seville, with
which it has regular bus
connections. González Byass,
c/Manuel María González,
Jerez de la Frontera (⊛www.
gonzalezbyass.es) run regular
tours.

mouldering in British cupboards are a world away from the lithe tang of a *fino* or bleached-dry *manzanilla* which dance on the palette and flirt coquettishly with tapas. In terms of sprucing up sherry's rather fusty image (at least outside Spain), González Byass have been leading the way with their rebranding of the famed *Tio Pepe*. Their cobbled lanes and crepuscular, vaulted cellars are among the oldest in Jerez, one of the most atmospheric – if touristy – places to sample a *fino* or an almond-nutty *amontillada* straight from the *bota* (sherry cask); you can even anoint your soles with some of their hallowed grapes during the September harvest. And if you're still hankering after the kind of tipple granny used to pour, nose out the chocolatey bitter-richness of a dry *oloroso* instead. Falstaff would approve.

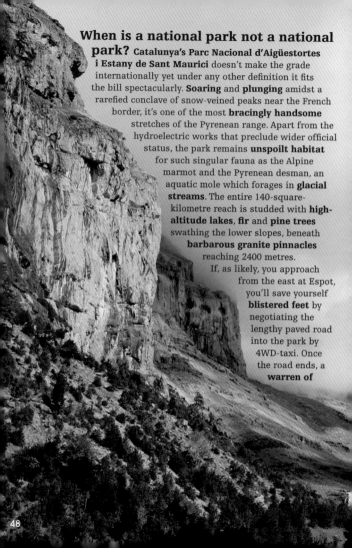

When is a national park not a national park?

Catalunya's Parc Nacional d'Aigüestortes i Estany de Sant Maurici doesn't make the grade internationally yet under any other definition it fits the bill spectacularly. **Soaring** and **plunging** amidst a rarefied conclave of snow-veined peaks near the French border, it's one of the most **bracingly handsome** stretches of the Pyrenean range. Apart from the hydroelectric works that preclude wider official status, the park remains **unspoilt habitat** for such singular fauna as the Alpine marmot and the Pyrenean desman, an aquatic mole which forages in **glacial streams**. The entire 140-square-kilometre reach is studded with **high-altitude lakes**, **fir** and **pine trees** swathing the lower slopes, beneath **barbarous granite pinnacles** reaching 2400 metres.

If, as likely, you approach from the east at Espot, you'll save yourself **blistered feet** by negotiating the lengthy paved road into the park by 4WD-taxi. Once the road ends, a **warren of** trails fans out from the **cobalt waters** of the Estany de Sant Maurici, with conveniently sited refuges at several of the intersections. Bisected by a main road and tunnel, the range then lunges westwards towards the equally impressive **Parque Nacional de Ordesa y Monte Perdido**. Inaugurated as far back as 1918, it gets the nod from UNESCO and the attention of climbers looking to tackle its **vertigo-stricken**, **Wild West-gone-alpine** canyons, which thunder with **glacial meltwater** in late spring. Those with a less adventurous head for heights can admire the **limestone strangeness** from the **depths of the Ordesa gorge**, where an unusual east–west orientation funnels in **damp Atlantic air** and supports **unexpectedly lush** vegetation; access is most common from the west, via the village of Torla. Some 10km further south **Añisclo**, an equally **breathtaking** and far less tourist-trodden canyon, can be accessed via a minor road turning off at Sarvisé. Sequestered in its **hulking gorge** wall is the hermitage of San Urbez, witness to the days when the national park was an **untrammelled wilderness**, home to mystics rather than wardens.

Hiking
in the
Pyrenees

21

need to know
Both parks are free but vehicular access to Aigüestortes is prohibited. See Ⓦwww.ordesa.net for up-to-date information on Ordesa's routes, transport and accommodation.

La Mezquita: a name that evokes the mystery and grace of Córdoba's famous monument so much more seductively than the English translation. It's been a while since the Great Mosque was used as such (1236 to be exact), but at one time it was not only the largest in the city – dwarfing a thousand others – but in all al-Andalus and nigh on the entire world.

Getting on for a millennium later, its hallucinatory interior still hushes the garrulous into silence and the jaded into awe, a dreamscape of candy-striped arches piled upon arches, sifting light from shadow. Since the Christians took over it's been mostly shadow, yet at one time the Mezquita's dense grove of recycled Roman columns was open to the sunlight, creating a generous, arboreal harmony with its courtyard and wider social environment. Today's visitors still enter through that same orange blossom compound, the Patio de los Naranjos, proceeding through the Puerta de las Palmas where they doff their cap rather than removing their shoes. As your eyes adjust to the gloom, you're

22

Marvelling inside the Mezquita

confronted with a jasper and marble forest, so constant, fluid and deceptively symmetrical in design that its ingenious system of secondary supporting arches barely registers, at least initially. Gradually, the resourcefulness of the Muslim architects sinks in, the way they improvised on the inadequacy of their salvaged pillars, inversely propping up the great weight of the roof arches and ceiling.

That first flush of wonder ebbs slightly once you stumble upon an edifice clearly out of step with the Moorish scheme of things, if gracious enough in its own right. In 1523, despite fierce local opposition, the more zealous Christians finally got their revenge by tearing out the Mosque's heart and erecting a Renaissance cathedral; Carlos V's verdict was damning: "you have destroyed something that was unique in the world." Thankfully they left intact the famous Mihrab, a prayer niche of sublime perfection braided by Byzantine mosaics and roofed with a single block of marble. Like the Mezquita itself, its beauty transcends religious difference.

need to know
Entry is €8, opening hours are typically convoluted; check ⓦwww.infocordoba.com for up-to-date details.

Into the Gypsy Mystic

fired up on *flamenco*

23

need to know

The Madrid *tablaos* charge between €25 and €35 per scrupulously professional performance. Seville's Bienal de Flamenco is held from mid-September through to mid-October.

With Diego El Cigala cleaning up at the Grammys, Catalan gypsy-punks Ojos de Brujo scooping a BBC Radio 3 World Music Award and Enrique Morente jamming with Sonic Youth (no, seriously) in Valencia, the socio-musico-cultural phenomenon that is Spanish flamenco has never been hotter. Like any improvisational art form (particularly jazz, with which it often shares a platform), it's most effective in the raw, on stage, as hands and heels thwack in virile syncopation, a guitar bleeds unfathomable flurries of notes and the dancer flaunts her disdain with a flourish of ruffled silk.

Those in serious search of the elusive *duende* may find themselves faced with a surfeit of touristy options, but genuine flamenco is almost always out there if you look hard enough. Madrid is home to producer extrodinaire Javier Limón and his new Casa Limón label, and boasts such famous *tablaos* as *Casa Patas*, *Corral de la Morería* and *El Corral de la Pacheca*, where Hollywood actors are as ubiquitous as the tiles and white linen. *Calle 54* is another Madrid institution, a latin jazz venue which often plays host to flamenco-centric artists: ace pianist Chano Domínguez is a regular and Cuba's Son De La Frontera appeared in 2005. Less pricey and more accommodating to the spirit of the *juerga* (spontaneous session) is the wonderful *La Soleá*, where both local and out-of-town enthusiasts test their mettle. Festivals include the annual Flamenco Pa'Tos charity bash and the new Suma Flamenca event which farms out shows to Madrid's wider *communidad*.

One of Spain's biggest festivals is Seville's La Bienal de Flamenco, an award-winning event. In the city itself, *Los Gallos* is one of the oldest *tablaos* but it's worth scouring the cobbled backstreets for *La Carbonería*, a former coal merchants where free flamenco pulls in a volubly appreciative scrum of locals and tourists, or heading to the old gyspy quarter of Triana where *barrio* hangouts like *Casa Anselma* exult in Seville's homegrown form, the *Sevillana*.

When you finally tire of sand, sea and mullet (that's the hairstyle, not the fish) the great thing about Spain is how easy it is to jump centuries in a few hours. Currently petitioning UNESCO for World Heritage status, Morella is the kind of living Knights Templar fantasy you're more likely to find in Castille or northern Portugal, yet it's located a mere 62km from the Mediterranean. Half the fun is actually getting there; after ascending from the anonymous sprawl of Castellón via plunging forests and queasy gradients, breaching the snow line and emerging into the liberating vastness of the *meseta* (plateau), you'll find Morella hunched inside beautifully preserved medieval walls, in the lee of a formidable castle, itself perched on a sheer, almost biblical outcrop of rock.

Even with the spring sunshine penetrating the town's precipitous, arcaded shadows, it's not too difficult to imagine how harsh and poverty-stricken the Franco-era winters were. Yet the locals are among the friendliest and most hospitable in Spain – the merest hint of political sympathies will likely inspire an endless supply of insight and *gratis* Gran Reserva. Talk with them for any length of time, and you'll soon get a sense of how fiercely proud the town is of its regional identity, to the extent that Spanish nationality itself is amorphous.

Nowadays the place thrives on a steady trickle of – largely Spanish – tourists, roaming narrow streets studded with gothic mansions (you can even lodge in one – the famous *Hotel Cardenal Ram* – for ridiculously reasonable rates), wooden balconies and restaurants serving the mouthwatering local speciality, *trufas negras* (black truffles). All roads ultimately lead to the castle, a truly magical site where crimson poppies and luminous butterflies flank dusty, serpentine paths and stupendous views, and the spiritual strata of past occupants – Ibero-Celts, Romans and Moors among them – lingers in every crumbling wall and cul de sac.

need to know

Morella is served by buses from both the resort town of Vinaròs and the regional capital of Castellón de la Plana. The castle is open daily, and a double room in **Hotel Cardenal Ram** costs around €75.

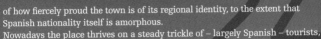

over the *meseta* to Morella

Playing with *fire* at Las Fallas

25

need to know

Las Fallas is held annually March 12-19, although things start hotting up from the beginning of the month. Accommodation is at a premium and often booked out months in advance. The Museo Faller is on Plaza de Monteolivete near the riverbed park,

While Wicker Man fever has only crept back into Britain over the last decade or so, Catholic Spain has traditionally held faster to old habits, syncretizing Saints' days with ancient seasonal rites.

The most famous – and noisiest – festival of all is Las Fallas: in mid-March Valencia's streets spontaneously combust in a riot of flame and firecrackers, ostensibly in celebration of St Joseph. As a recent local article put it: "Gunpowder is like blood for any Valencian Festival", and that goes double for Las Fallas; it's (barely) controlled pyromania on a scale unrivalled anywhere in Europe, a festival where the neighbourhood firemen are on overtime and beauty sleep is in short supply.

If you're not still partying from the night before, a typical Fallas day will see you rudely awakened at 7am by the galumphing cacophony of a brass band (perhaps it's no coincidence that the *shawm* – an ancestor of the oboe – was originally employed by Arab armies as an early form of psychological warfare). By 2pm sharp, you'll likely be part of the baying mob in the Plaza Ayuntamiento, standing gape-mouthed in anticipation of the Mascletà, a daily round of colour and seismic blast. The fallas themselves are huge satirical tableaux peopled by *ninots*, or allegorical figures – everyone from voluptuous harlots to George W. Bush – painstakingly crafted out of wood, wax, papier-mâché and cardboard. They're exhibited by their respective Casals Faller – the grass roots community houses which run the festival – during nightly street parties, before all 500 of them literally go up in smoke; the *Cremà* (the burning) represents the festival's climax, kicking off at midnight on March 19.

a riot of flame and firecrackers

If the heady aroma of cordite, wood-fired paella, *buñuelos* (pumpkin fritters) and industrial strength drinking chocolate is all too much for you, you can always view the *fallas* that got away (one gets a reprieve each year) in the quieter – and saner – environs of the city's Museu Faller.

25

Ultimate
experiences
Spain
miscellany

1 Duende

Duende is a quintessentially Spanish, supposedly **untranslatable** concept, originally referring to a supernatural fairy or spirit and still widely used in this sense in Latin America. In Spain, the term has come to signify a moment of cathartic ecstasy in art, particularly flamenco and bullfighting (if bullfighting can be called art), when the artist or performer, and by extension the audience, is consumed with the raw, volatile energy of pure creation in the face of death.

2 Food

Eating out in Spain is a question of better late than never, with restaurants empty until at least 9pm and not filling up until 10pm onwards. Tapas grazing is a great way to acclimatize.

▶▶ **Top five tapas bars**

Barbiana c/Albareda 11, Seville. Thunderous conversation and flaky-fresh Costa de la Luz fish.

Cal Pep Plaça de les Olles 8, Barcelona. Seafood landmark with queues of loyal Catalans.

La Casa Del Abuelo c/Victoria 12, Madrid. Forget the mantra of consumer choice; this place only serves one dish – prawns – and they've spent 100 years doing so.

La Cuchara de San Telmo c/31 de Agosto 28, in San Sebastian. Pintxo sized portions of trendy Basque gastronomy for a few euros and no fuss.

La Taberna Del Gourmet in Alicante. Pricey but immaculate food, organic wine and Spanish tradition without the brusqueness.

▶▶ **Five foods to try**

Churros Strips of fried dough dunked in viscous chocolate.
Jamón serrano Cured ham, perfected in Extremadura.
Paella Valencia's famous saffron-flavoured rice and seafood.
Pimientos de Padrón Unpredictably hot Galician peppers.
Tortilla Egg and potato omelette.

3 Festival calendar

Festival	When and where
Cabalgata de Reyes Three Wise Men showering the crowds with sweets	January 5–6; countrywide
Carnaval Bacchanalian revelry	February/March; countrywide, particularly Cádiz, Sitges, Águilas and Santa Cruz de Tenerife
Las Fallas Celebration of patron saint St Joseph with much partying and burning of effigies	March 12–19; Valencia
Moros y Cristianos Re-enactment of Christian vs Moor battles	April 22–24; mostly eastern Spain
Burial of the Sardine Fishy funeral	Easter Saturday; Murcia
Feria de Abril	last week in April; Seville
Romería del Rocío Pentecostal pilgrimage from all corners of Andalucía	weekend of the 7th week after Easter; El Rocío
Corpus Christi	May or June; countrywide, particularly Toleda, Cádiz, Valencia and Granada
Danza de los Zancos Stilt dancing for Mary Magdalene	June 21–23; Anguiano, La Rioja
San Juan Fireworks and jumping over bonfires	June 23–24; countrywide, notably Alicante and Las Palmas
San Fermín Notorious running of the bulls	July 6–14; Pamplona
Fiesta de Santa Marta de Ribarteme Bizarre festival of near death experiences	July 29; Las Nieves, Galicia
La Tomatina World-famous tomato fight	last Wednesday in August; Buñol
La Virgen del Pilar	October 12; Zaragoza
Nochevieja Auld Lang Syne Spanish-style:	December 31; everywhere

4 Spanish dynasties

Habsburg

Carlos I	1516–56
Felipe II	1556–98
Felipe III	1598–1621
Felipe IV	1621–65
Carlos II	1665–1700

Bourbon

Felipe V	1700–24 and 1724–46
Louis I	1724
Ferdinand VI	1746–59
Carlos III	1759–88
Carlos IV	1788–1808
Ferdinand VII	1808
Ferdinand VII	1814–33
Isabella II	1833–68
Alfonso XII	1874–85
Alfonso XIII	1886–1931
Juan Carlos I	1975–present

Other

Joseph Bonaparte	1808–13
Francisco Serrano y Domínguez (regent)	1869–70
Amadeo I of Savoy	1870–73
First Republic	1873–74
Second Republic	1931–39
Franco's Dictatorship	1939–75

"There are two kinds of man: the ones who make history and the ones who endure it."

Novelist Camilo José Cela

5 Beautiful beaches

Bolonia Costa de la Luz, Tarifa Relentless wind keeps the crowds away at this remote, very low-key quasi-resort, flanked by the Roman ruins of Baelo Claudia.

Calblanque Murcia Wild, mercifully underdeveloped series of beaches fringing a nature reserve just south of Cabo de Palos.

Playa de los Genoveses Cabo de Gata, Almería Flaxen sand and mineral-rich desert inside Spain's driest natural park.

Playa de Oyambre Comillas, Cantabria A great white escape from Santander, popular with surfers.

Xilloi O Vecedo, Lugo Crystal clear, blue-flag bay buffered by emerald cliffs.

6 Spanish territories past and present

▶▶ Spanish enclaves

Never far from the headlines, **Ceuta** and **Melilla** are Spanish-held territories, retained after Moroccan independence in 1956, located on Morocco's northern coast. They are ringed by hi-tech security fences designed to keep out sub-Saharan migrants and both have military bases on them. The nearby, uninhabited islands of Peñón de Vélez de la Gomera, Peñón de Alhumcemas, Islas Chafarinas, Isla de Alborán and Isla Perejil are also sovereign Spanish territory, disputed by Morocco. In July 2002, Isla Perejil witnessed a rare military stand-off as Spanish commandos removed a group of Moroccan navy cadets.

▶▶ Lesser-spotted former Spanish colonies

Western Sahara
Equatorial Guinea
Guam
The Caroline Islands
Palau

7 Religion

Although church attendance has **declined** sharply in recent years, Spain remains overwhelmingly Roman Catholic, a religion that defined the fifteenth-century Reconquista over the Moors and the formation of the Spanish state. It also played a pivotal role in the Civil War, with Nationalist forces claiming to be fighting for God and Christian civilization (ring any bells?). Franco's subsequent dictatorship remained closely tied to the Church, heavily subsidizing its activities and with him personally appointing bishops. **Opus Dei**, the secretive Catholic society founded in Spain in the late 1920s, was also the subject of recent scrutiny after being featured in Dan Brown's best-selling novel, *The Da Vinci Code*.

The country's sizeable **Jewish** and **Muslim** populations were forcibly expelled in the late fifteenth and early sixteenth centuries (Spain only established diplomatic relations with Israel in 1986), but Islam is now the country's second largest faith, with around one million – largely North African – Muslims.

8 Tourism

At the height of Spain's 1960s and 1970s **tourism revolution**, Málaga's Civil Hospital boasted a psychiatric ward dedicated to male teenage waiters literally culture-shocked after their transition from rural *pueblo* to Costa del Sol fleshpot.

Since the death of Franco, Spain has consistently been one of the most visited countries in the world, second only to France in terms of global tourist numbers. Tourism currently accounts for 12 percent of GDP, with increasing numbers of travellers avoiding beach holidays in favour of rural destinations and city breaks.

9 Five of the best books on Spain

Homage to Catalonia, George Orwell. Gripping first-person account of the Spanish Civil War, unflinching in its portrayal of internecine conflict.

The New Spaniards, John Hooper. Exhaustive and perceptive analysis of pretty much every facet of life in post-Franco Spain, though badly in need of updating.

Our Lady of the Sewers, Paul Richardson. With a brief "to sieve out the ancient, perverse and eccentric from the new, nice and normal" how could he fail? Engrossing, casually hilarious and outrageously well informed.

Sacred Roads, Nicholas Shrady. A book on global pilgrimages rather than Spain, but Shrady's winter journey along the *camino francés* remains one of the most lucid contemporary accounts in print.

Voices of the Old Sea, Norman Lewis. With tender humour and pristine prose, Lewis recreates the lost world of post-war peasant and fishing communities soon to be eclipsed by tourism.

10 The Basques

The Basques are widely recognized as being the oldest ethnic group in Europe, with archaeological findings suggesting a continuous presence for more than 30,000 years. Known as **Euskal Herria** to the Basque people, the Basque region covers the three Basque provinces in Spain: Gipuzkoa, Bizkaia and Alava, together with Navarra and part of southwestern France. Their language, Euskarra, bears no relation to the Indo-European languages that spawned Latin, Castilian, Catalan and French, and some linguists have claimed to show an even older genesis by highlighting vocabulary relating to the stone age, a theory seemingly backed up by homogenous blood type.

The Spanish state's battle with paramilitary Basque nationalist group ETA, or **Euskadi Ta Askatasuna** (Euskadi and Freedom), has been going on since the early 1960s. Initially formed out of resistance to the cultural repression and brutality of the Franco regime, the group went on to target academics, businessmen, journalists and tourists. After an earlier ceasefire in 1998, the group finally declared a "permanent ceasefire" in March 2006, before announcing six months later that they would continue with armed struggle until Basque independence. Negotiations with José Luis Rodríguez Zapatero's government are nevertheless ongoing.

11 Sport

Spain is a nation of **fútbol** obsessives, home to a league that has long been the envy of Europe. Barcelona and Real Madrid remain two of the biggest names in world football yet – with typical contrariness – the national team are perennial underachievers; their best showing to date was fourth place in the 1950 World Cup.

A 2003 survey by the University of Navarra ranked Spain as the **third most sedentary nation** in the EU, with only Belgium and Portugal doing less exercise.

12 The high life

Spain is the second highest country in Europe after Switzerland, with most of the land lying above 500m.

▶▶ Five highest mountains in Spain

Teide (Tenerife)	3718m
Mulhacén (Sierra Nevada)	3479m
Aneto (Pyrenees)	3404m
Veleta (Sierra Nevada)	3392m
Llardana (Pyrenees)	3375m

Spain boasted the most southerly **glacier** in Europe as recently as 1913, when the Corral de la Veleta in the Sierra Nevada finally melted.

13 Las Españas: Spain's Autonomous Communities

Throughout Iberian history, **regionalism** has exerted a powerful and often bitter counterweight to national unity; the Basques and Catalans have been particularly tenacious in fighting for self-determination. Following the demise of Franco and his repressively centralist regime, Spain's regions were gradually granted varying degrees of self-government.

Seventy-four percent of the population speak **Castilian** Spanish as their first language, seventeen percent speak variants of Catalan, seven percent Galician and two percent Basque. Road signs will often be in the regional language as well as (or instead of) Castilian. The **Catalan language** is more widely spoken than several national European languages, and is heard outside Catalunya in the Balearic Islands, Andorra, the French department of Pyrénées Orientales and as far afield as the Sardinian town of Alghero.

▸▸ Biggest regions

Region	Population	Languages Spoken
Andalucía	7.85 million	Castilian
Catalunya	6.99 million	Catalan, Castilian, Aranese
Madrid	5.96 million	Castilian
Valencia	4.69 million	Valencian, Castilian
Galicia	2.76 million	Galician, Castilian

14 Politics

In western European terms, **Spanish democracy** is still young, only fully emerging in the late 1970s. Its constitutional monarchy allows for a president elected by parliament. Save for a brief period of government by the centre-right Partido Popular, modern politics have been dominated by the PSOE, roughly equivalent to British New Labour. The party won back their majority in 2004 after PP leader José María Aznar's hugely unpopular support for the Iraq war and his cabinet's handling of the 2004 Madrid train bombings.

In June 2005 Spain became the third country in the EU to legalize **gay marriage**, a move supported by over 70 percent of the Spanish population.

"You can't bomb a people just in case."
Prime Minister José Luis Rodríguez Zapatero

15 Five great Spanish films

Viridiana (1961). Luis Buñuel's Palme D'Or-winning masterpiece, torched by the Franco regime.

The Spirit of the Beehive (1973). Mesmeric one-off, set in the barren plains of Castille in the aftermath of the Civil War.

Open Your Eyes (1997). Alejandro Amenábar's mindbending thriller, re-made as *Vanilla Sky* by Cameron Crowe.

Lovers of the Arctic Circle (1999). An absorbing, very Spanish love story, typical of director Julio Bardem's labyrinthine, game-of-chance style.

Talk To Her (2002). The richest and most acclaimed of all Pedro Almodóvar's films.

16 The Spanish Civil War

A bloody prelude to World War II, the Spanish Civil War broke out in July 1936 and lasted for almost three years, until beleaguered Republican forces surrendered on April 1, 1939. An uneasy coalitin of liberals, socialists, Communists and anarchists had fought alongside the army, loyal to the leftist Popular Front government, against a Nationalist uprising by **General Francisco Franco**. He was supported by the landed gentry, Carlist monarchists, fascists and the majority of Catholic priests. The fact that the Nationalists were aided by Italy, Germany and Portugal (albeit strategically), and the Republicans by the USSR, also made it a prelude to the Cold War, while the International Brigades (foreign volunteers fighting on the Republican side) demonstrated the passions aroused by the conflict worldwide. Franco's victory inaugurated almost four decades of dictatorship, isolation and repression, shaping modern Spanish life and politics.

17 Rivers

Seville is the only inland river port for ocean-going traffic in Spain, accessed by the Guadalquivir river.

River	Starts	Ends	Length in km
Tajo	Albarracín mountains	Lisbon, Atlantic	1,038
Ebro	Pico de los Tres Mares, Cantabria	Tarragona, Mediterranean	910
Duero	Sierra de Urbión, Soria province	Porto, Atlantic	897
Guadiana	La Mancha Plateau	Gulf of Cadiz, Atlantic	778
Guadalquivir	Cazorla mountain range	Gulf of Cadiz, Atlantic	657

18 Los Toros

Although a common sight on bar TVs across the country during bullfighting season (March–Oct), within Spain it attracts less **aficionados** and more **controversy** than might be imagined, at least in comparison to a spectator sport like football. It's been outlawed in the Canary Islands since 1991 and Barcelona recently declared itself an "anti-bullfighting city", although these policies are generally regarded as at least partly influenced by the desire to emphasize cultural distance from Madrid.

"Don't bother about being modern. Unfortunately it is the one thing that, whatever you do, you cannot avoid."

Salvador Dalí

19   Velázquez and Picasso

Spanish art is dominated by the legacy of **Diego Velázquez**, the seventeenth-century painter who furthered the limits of portraiture and paved the way for both Realism and Impressionism. His most famous work, **Las Meninas**, is regarded by many artists and critics as the greatest canvas ever painted. In 1957 **Pablo Picasso** produced 44 interpretations of *Las Meninas*, deconstructing the individual portraits that make up Velázquez's work. These are all on display at the **Museu Picasso in Barcelona.**

"Art washes away from the soul the dust of everyday life."

Pablo Picasso

20   Five classics of Spanish literature

Blood Wedding Federico García Lorca. Lorca's searing, *duende*-drenched landmark, based on a true story.

Don Quixote Miguel de Cervantes. Universally acclaimed classic of Spanish literature, charting the chivalrous whims of the deluded hero and his dimwitted sidekick.

The Family Of Pascual Duarte Camilo José Cela. The Nobel Prize-winner's most compelling novel, confessing the brutal, nihilistic life of an Extremaduran peasant.

Requiem for a Spanish Peasant Ramón Sender. Vivid and unflinching account of an idealist betrayed by his parish priest during the Civil War.

Winter In Lisbon Antonio Muñoz Molina. Evocative, prize-winning jazz noir, sifting memory, identity and infatuation. Made into a rarely seen film starring Dizzy Gillespie.

"In Spain the dead are more alive than the dead of any other country in the world."

Federico García Lorca

21 Ibiza

After almost two decades as a global house-music Mecca, the Balearic island of Ibiza is coming full circle with a return to the bohemian spirit of the 1960s. As the authorities look to finally put an end to 24-7 revelling, the decline of superclub culture has been accompanied by a rise in live music, non-superstar DJs and laidback partying. The legendary **Manumission** has responded with Ibiza Rocks, hosting bands like Kaiser Chiefs and The Editors, and tellingly, while the 2006 season saw the island's airport handle record visitor numbers, the biggest increases in revenue were in lower key resorts like **Santa Eulària**.

"It's better to arrive at the right time than to be invited."

Spanish proverb

22 Wildlife

The **Iberian Lynx**, one of Spain's most graceful wild animals, is the most endangered big cat in the world as well as the most endangered carnivorous species in Europe. Just over a hundred adults survive, largely in two pockets of Andalucía, one near Andujar in the north of the province, and one on the fringes of the Coto de Doñana national park. Hunting, disease-ravaged rabbit populations and road traffic have all contributed to the dwindling numbers, although a captive breeding programme may yet prevent extinction.

23 Iberian ingenuity

Perhaps the most famous of Spanish inventions is the **six-string guitar**, although they've also brought us the submarine, graded lenses for glasses and the humble lollipop. More recently, we have the Spanish to thank for celebrity bible *Hello!*, a spin-off from its Iberian forebear, *¡Hola!*.

24 The siesta

"Waking up earlier won't make the sun rise faster."
Spanish proverb

Contrary to popular belief, the Spanish siesta, or early afternoon nap, originated in the Alentejo region of Portugal. Although the practice is being eroded due to economic demands, in most of Spain you'll still find **nothing doing** between 2 and 5pm. The shutdown is generally spent over a long lunch rather than in the sack, but a recent national commission blamed the lengthy lunch hour for sleep deprivation (due to working later at night and going to bed later), attendant low productivity and even increased physical and mental illness. It looks unlikely, however, that leisurely afternoons will be abandoned with any great enthusiasm, and the Portuguese have even formed a pressure group to defend them.

25 Five great summer music festivals

Castell de Peralada Festival World-class opera and classical music in Peralada castle near Gerona, from mid-July to mid-August.

Festival Ortigueira Long-running folk festival held in the wilds of northern Galicia each July, recently featuring flamenco crossover talents La Negra and Niño Josele.

FIB (Festival Internacional de Benicàssim) A beachside location in late July or early August has made this one of Europe's hippest events. Radiohead, Belle and Sebastian, Air, the Pixies, Nick Cave and the Strokes have all appeared over the last decade.

Jazzaldia Forty years and still going strong, San Sebastián's July jazz festival has hosted the likes of Herbie Hancock, Erykah Badu and Keith Jarrett as well as Brazilian legends Caetano Veloso and Gilberto Gil.

Sónar Electronic music and multimedia jamboree held in Barcelona in mid-June, with Goldfrapp, DJ Shadow, Giles Peterson and Linton Kwesi Johnson all guesting recently.

25

Ultimate
experiences
Spain
small print

Spain
The complete experience

ROUGH GUIDES – don't just travel

We hope you've been inspired by the experiences in this book. To us, they sum up what makes Spain such an extraordinary and stimulating place to travel. There are 24 other books in the 25 Ultimate Experiences series, each conceived to whet your appetite for travel and for everything the world has to offer. As well as covering the globe, the 25s series also includes books on **Journeys, World Food, Adventure Travel, Places to Stay, Ethical Travel, Wildlife Adventures** and **Wonders of the World**.

When you start planning your trip, Rough Guides' new-look guides, maps and phrasebooks are the ultimate companions. For 25 years we've been refining what makes a good guidebook and we now include more colour photos and more information – on average 50% more pages – than any of our competitors. Just look for the sky-blue spines.

Rough Guides don't just travel – we also believe in getting the most out of life without a passport. Since the publication of the bestselling Rough Guides to **The Internet** and **World Music**, we've brought out a wide range of lively and authoritative guides on everything from **Climate Change** to **Hip-Hop**, from **MySpace** to **Film Noir** and from **The Brain** to **The Rolling Stones**.

Publishing information

Rough Guide 25 Ultimate experiences Spain Published May 2007 by Rough Guides Ltd, 80 Strand, London WC2R 0RL
345 Hudson St, 4th Floor,
New York, NY 10014, USA
14 Local Shopping Centre, Panchsheel Park, New Delhi 110017, India
Distributed by the Penguin Group
Penguin Books Ltd,
80 Strand, London WC2R 0RL
Penguin Group (USA)
375 Hudson Street, NY 10014, USA
Penguin Group (Australia)
250 Camberwell Road, Camberwell,
Victoria 3124, Australia
Penguin Books Canada Ltd,
10 Alcorn Avenue, Toronto, Ontario,
Canada M4V 1E4
Penguin Group (NZ)
67 Apollo Drive, Mairangi Bay, Auckland 1310, New Zealand

Printed in China
© Rough Guides 2007
No part of this book may be reproduced in any form without permission from the publisher except for the quotation of brief passages in reviews.
80pp
A catalogue record for this book is available from the British Library
ISBN: 978-1-84353-828-8
The publishers and authors have done their best to ensure the accuracy and currency of all the information in **Rough Guide 25 Ultimate experiences Spain**, however, they can accept no responsibility for any loss, injury, or inconvenience sustained by any traveller as a result of information or advice contained in the guide.

1   3   5   7   9   8   6   4   2

Rough Guide credits

Editor: Alice Park
Design & picture research: Michelle Bhatia
Cartography: Maxine Repath, Katie Lloyd-Jones

Cover design: Diana Jarvis, Chloë Roberts
Production: Aimee Hampson, Katherine Owers
Proofreader: Sarah Eno

The authors

Brendon Griffin (all Experiences except 7; Miscellany) has contributed to Rough Guides on Spain, Portugal, West Africa, Central America and Bolivia.
Martin Dunford (Experience 7) is a co-founder of Rough Guides and has authored Rough Guides to Brussels, Amsterdam, New York, Rome and Italy.

Picture credits

Cover Alhambra, Granada © Simeone Huber/Getty Images
2 Seagulls follow fishing trawler off the coast of Galicia © Alex Segre/Alamy
5 Vineyard near Laguardia, Rioja © Cephas Picture Library/Alamy
8–9 Bilbao Museo Guggenheim © Bildarchiv Monheim

GmbH /Alamy
10–11 Bernabéu Stadium © Carmona/Corbis
soccer ball illustration © istockphoto
Real Madrid's forward Ruud Van Nistelrooy © Juan Carlos Cardenas/epa/Corbis
Real Madrid players Ruud Van Nistelrooy (L) and Fabio Cannavaro © Juan Carlos Cardenas/EFE/Corbis

Real Madrid player Fabio Cannavaro © Stephane
Reix/For Picture/Corbis
Real Madrid's David Beckham © Victor Fraile/Reuters/
Corbis
12-13 Plaza del Tossal, Valencia © Kevin Foy/Alamy
14-15 Court of the Myrtles, The Alhambra, Granada ©
Eddi Boehnke/zefa/Corbis
16-17 Statue of Francisco Pizarro, Trujillo, Extremadura
© Jordi Cami/ Alamy
18-19 Hikers in Cares Gorge, Picos de Europa ©
PICIMPACT/Corbis
20-21 Bulls chasing runners during San Fermin festival,
Pamplona © Vincent West/Reuters/Corbis
22-23 Ski resort, Sierra Nevada, Andalucía © Hemis
/Alamy
24-25 Seagulls follow fishing trawler off the coast of
Galicia © Alex Segre/Alamy
Mussel fisherman works in El Globe, Galicia © Owen
Franken/ Corbis
Barnacle fishing in Galicia © Prat Thierry/ Corbis Sygma
Barnacle fishing in Galicia © Prat Thierry/ Corbis Sygma
26-27 Dalí Museum at Figueres, Catalonia © Tim
Cuff/Alamy
28-29 A group of storks on a harvested rice field, Isla
Mayor, Seville © Felipe Rodriguez/Alamy
30-31 Film set of old Western building, Texas Hollywood
Studios, Almería © M. J. Mayo/Alamy
32-33 Vineyard near Laguardia, Rioja © Cephas
Picture Library/Alamy
Vina Real in barrels in cellar of CVNE Haro La Rioja ©
Cephas Picture Library/Alamy
Ysios winery Spain © John Warburton-Lee/Alamy
34-35 Woman in traditional black clothes, Rio de Onor
© B.A.E. Inc./Alamy
Traditional stone buildings with wooden doors, Rio de
Onor © B.A.E. Inc. / Alamy
36-37 Olives in a bowl © DK Images
Salpicon de mariscos (seafood salad) © DK Images
Meat balls (albondigas) © DK Images
Patrons enjoy tapas in a bar, Madrid © Owen Franken/
Corbis
Salmon, mussels and caviar © Cesar Rangel/AFP/Getty
Images Getty Images

38-39 Gaudí chimney, Parc Güell © DK Images
Gaudí's Casa Milá chimneys © Ella Milroy/Departure
Lounge DK Images
Close up of Antoni Gaudí's Lizard fountain, Park Güell ©
Alison Cornford-Matheson istockphoto
Gaudí's Sagrada Familia, Eixample © Ella Milroy/
Departure Lounge DK Images
40-41 Nazarenos (Nazarenes), members of cofradía
(religious brotherhood) of Quinta Angustia, Holy
Thursday. Photograph by Damien Simonis © Rough
Guides
Paso (float) with Virgin Mary, cofradía of El Señor del
Gran Poder, Good Friday morning. Photograph by
Damien Simonis © Rough Guides
Nazarenos (Nazarenes), members of cofradía of Monte
Sión, Holy Thursday. Photograph by Damien Simonis ©
Rough Guides
Young member of cofradía of La O, which parades
from Triana on Good Friday evening. Photograph by
Damien Simonis © Rough Guides
42-43 Windsurfing in Tarifa © isifa Image Service
s.r.o./Alamy
44-45 Pilgrims stand in front of the Cathedral of
Santiago de Compostela © Miguel Vidal/Reuters/
Corbis
Pilgrims on the Camino de Santiago © Chris Howarth/
Alamy
Shell detail, symbol of Santiago de Compostela ©
Jacques Pavlovsky/Sygma/Corbis
46-47 Man pouring sherry, Jerez © Gregor M. Schmid/
Corbis
48-49 Ordesa National Park, Spain. Clouds over Anisclo
Canyon © Francesc Muntada/Corbis
50-51 Mezquita, Córdoba, Andalucía © Mark
Zybler/Alamy
52-53 Flamenco dancers perform in Madrid © Danita
Delimont/Alamy
54-55 Castle at Morella with the village below ©
Hemis/Alamy
56-57 Beginning of Cremá Falla del Convento de
Jerusalén, March 19, Valencia. Photograph by Damien
Simonis © Rough Guides
58 Gaudí chimney, Parc Güell © DK Images

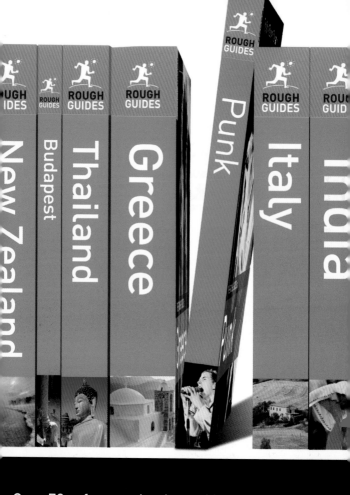

Over 70 reference books and hundreds of travel
guides, maps & phrasebooks that cover the world

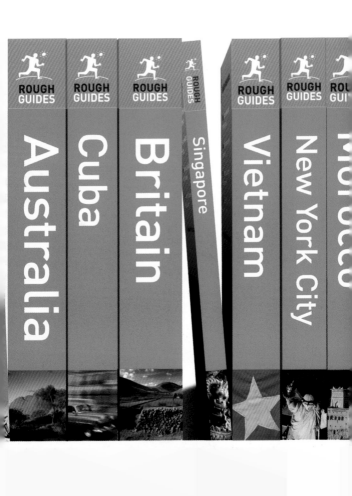

ROUGH GUIDES

Australia

ROUGH GUIDES

Cuba

ROUGH GUIDES

Britain

ROUGH GUIDES

Singapore

ROUGH GUIDES

Vietnam

ROUGH GUIDES

New York City

ROUGH GUIDES

Morocco

Index